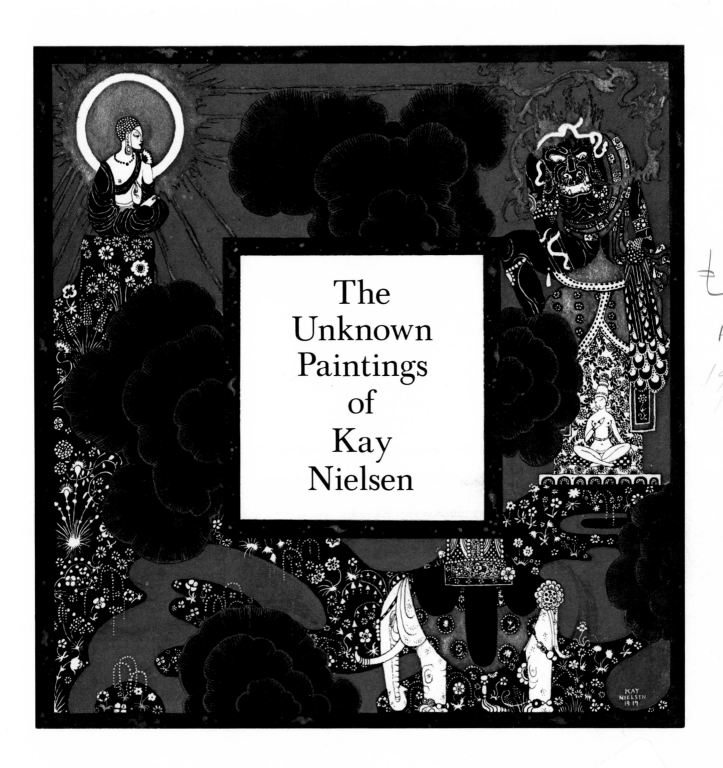

The Unknown Paintings of Kay Nielsen

£5 —
Art
19/8

The Unknown Paintings of Kay Nielsen

Edited by David Larkin

With an Elegy by
Hildegarde Flanner

A Peacock Press/Bantam Book
Toronto · New York · London

An original PEACOCK PRESS/BANTAM BOOK

THE UNKNOWN PAINTINGS OF KAY NIELSEN

© 1977 Bantam Books, Inc.

Elegy © 1977 Hildegarde Flanner Monhoff

All rights reserved.

PRINTING HISTORY:
First Edition: March, 1977

This book may not be reproduced in whole or in part, by mimeograph
or by any other means, without permission in writing. For information,
address: Peacock Press, Bearsville, New York 12409, U.S.A.

Bantam Books are published by Bantam Books, Inc. Its trademark,
consisting of the words "Bantam Books" and the portrayal of a bantam,
is registered in the United States Patent Office and in other countries.
Marca Registrada. Bantam Books, Inc., 666 Fifth Avenue, New York,
New York 10019, U.S.A.

Published simultaneously in the United States and Canada

PRINTED IN THE UNITED STATES OF AMERICA
by Regensteiner Press

Publisher's Note

Kay Rasmus Nielsen was born in Copenhagen in 1886, of distinguished parents. His mother, Oda Larssen, was a notable actress and his father, Professor Martinius Nielsen, also a classical actor, eventually became Director of the Royal Danish Theater. This theatrical and intellectual background exposed young Nielsen to a cultured, well-mannered and privileged world. Privately tutored from the age of twelve, he finally went to Paris to continue his study of art. Although strongly influenced by the morbid clarity of Beardsley and the spare, exquisitely terse Japanese woodcut landscapes, Kay Nielsen's powerful style resulted in work which was uniquely his own. As a mature artist, exhibitions of his paintings for several books were arranged in London, which had become a Mecca for the finest illustrators, and in New York.

Back in Denmark he collaborated with Johannes Poulsen in spectacular productions for which Nielsen did the elaborately beautiful costumes and set designs. This partnership eventually took Nielsen to Hollywood, where, among other things, he did the Bald Mountain sequence for Disney's "Fantasia". But by this time illustration had gone out of fashion, and Nielsen's style, in particular, was too special and sophisticated for an increasingly plastic world. The commissions became fewer and fewer. Even in his native Denmark, to which he and his wife briefly returned in desperation, Nielsen's art was no longer wanted. The Golden Age of Illustrators had passed, and in 1957, in Los Angeles, Kay Nielsen died in artistic obscurity. But not without friends.

He and his wife Ulla had formed close and lasting relationships in their adopted country. Those who loved the indomitable Danish couple also loved and respected the work of Kay Nielsen. After his death, Ulla gave to Hildegarde and Frederick Monhoff the illustrations Nielsen had done years before for a never published edition of "A Thousand and One Nights". The Monhoffs made many efforts to get these exquisite paintings placed, or to find some arrangement which would create the memorial to Nielsen that they now sought. They were frustrated. No museum, even in Denmark, would accept the paintings. But the Monhoffs carefully preserved and treasured their precious charge, until eventually, the quality of Nielsen's work was once again recognized.

The public, no less than the publishers of this book, owes a debt to Frederick Monhoff and to Hildegarde Flanner Monhoff for their faith in the artist and their devoted care in preserving his work. It is a very great pleasure to acknowledge that debt and to discharge a small part of it by publishing these reproductions of the unknown work of Kay Nielsen. Mrs. Monhoff has selected the Los Angeles County Museum of Art to administer a fund set up from the proceeds earned by this volume, for the benefit of promising artists.

The "Elegy" by Hildegarde Flanner Monhoff which follows speaks eloquently of the quality of the relationship between the Monhoffs and the Nielsens — a relationship which has been instrumental in at last bringing recognition to the memory of Kay Nielsen, and no less to gallant Ulla, who loved and supported and upheld him.

David Larkin
London

Ian and Betty Ballantine
Bearsville, New York

An Elegy

When I was young and attending a school for girls in the middle western city where my family lived it was my greatest pleasure to come home of an afternoon, done with arithmetic and Latin, free at last to lie on the library couch with graham crackers and a banana, wide open on my hiked-up knees the most beautiful book in our house. To me, the most beautiful book on earth, "East of the Sun and West of the Moon: Old tales from the North", illustrated by the Danish artist Kay Nielsen. The stories had the elemental appeal of ancient legends and the courtliness of being told often by people who loved them, but it was the enchantment of the illustrations that I threw myself into after a day of tedious lessons. I was too ignorant to know anything about the artist or his reputation although the size of the book carried a worldly importance. In my young way I was certain that he was a creator inspired and flawlessly on fire as snow may be on fire with the northern lights. It is good when we are young to be so possessed. And through the pages moved the heavy, pale stallions, the lean and lovely women, the pure, muscular knights of the Nielsen imagination, a company whose joys and sufferings lifted me straight up from the printed page into late afternoons of heaven. It was a folk-heaven of romance and danger, of odd evils and cranky virtues, of love and the marvel of proud regal gender, but no sex. Under the long, sweeping garments of Art Nouveau as within the emblazoned armor of these pictures there was no rage of the flesh.

I was brought up a religious child, but the illustrations of Bible stories showed a young man too sweetly moral to have mystery or authority, and the question sometimes asked, "Do you know Jesus?" held no interest for me. But if any one had had the insight to ask, "Do you know the Lindworm?" with what elated terror I could have cried, "I do!", and opened the book to the page where the tall serpentine prince, the redeemed and redeemer, stood in his coils and commanded a kingdom with his hard red mouth.

In almost any group of adult people today there are one or two who knew the work of Kay Nielsen when they were young. Then, they would have known him ardently and doubtless mispronounced his name. Kay is Kigh. Not he, but his young admirers might have been guilty of excess. He would have made them happy and lonely and inarticulate. Yet he had passed into obscurity, become something nostalgic, of childhood memories, not of the present.

Until in May, 1975, there occurred a publishing event that provided both pleasure and surprise to people who knew his work and had not foreseen any early renascence of interest in it beyond what the greeting card industry has been promoting on the west coast and in England. KAY NIELSEN (A Peacock Press/Bantam Book, edited by David Larkin, with an introduction by Keith Nicholson) gave back to public view forty of his most characteristic designs selected from now rarely found volumes of his career. These meticulous yet highly imaginative paintings have, in their deliberate charm and exquisite refinement, no relationship to contemporary tendencies or tastes. The consequent neglect through which they have survived has been, as a matter of fact, a jealous neglect maintained by his admirers who never forgot him but had the good sense to let him be, and knowing how completely out of step with our times he was, did not betray him to inevitable indifference. He belonged with many others to what has been called "the Golden Age of Illustration", an age that for more than half a century has continued to have academic respect but no enthusiastic attention. A substantial list of formerly popular illustrators is now being issued by Peacock/Bantam Books whose directors, Ian and Betty Ballantine, believe the time has come for their restoration. If this is so, then in the case at least of Kay Nielsen, the time has come for what I shall call An Elegy. There are not many people still living who knew him, and I am one of them and have a conscience about him. It is proper to set down what I remember. Proper, but not easy, because reticence and good manners such as he practised do not focus sharply, and what comes to mind is a gentle figure in soft light. Moreover, if this memoir is dominated by Ulla, his wife, that is because that is the way it was in life, and also the way he would have preferred it in memory.

Since the time when I had first known the Nielsen illustrations more than a quarter of a century had passed when I was singled out by a curious destiny to be unique, not in myself unique, but by a caprice of circumstances made the recipient of odd personal fortune, so shaped by coincidence that it was hard to believe. I was married to Frederick Monhoff, an architect and artist, living in a suburban community in the foothills of southern California. These recollections begin during the second war. The old garden in which we lived was surrounded by a tall hedge of Monterey cypress. From the street it was difficult to obtain any glimpse of what was within, including ourselves. I became aware that someone, when passing, tried to peer in, and at length, in a brief scurry, I caught him at it. It was not a man, but a woman, somehow European-looking and leading two Scottie dogs, then faddish, on a double leash. There was tone about her and that double leash and the well-groomed dogs. She quickly took off down the street. On other days I heard her talking to the Scotties, but I could not make out what she said. She and the dogs were not speaking English.

Then one day, accompanied by a distinguished man, she came to call on my family. Our callers were new-comers living around the corner. They were from Denmark, and it is the courteous Danish custom, we learned, to present oneself to people established nearby. When I heard that the distinguished man was Kay Nielsen, whom I had revered for most of my life and who had, in an eerie way an influence on my mind, I was overcome by shyness and a childish feeling of unworthiness, and by the overwhelming strangeness of his having been led from the limitlessness of the earth and his native snows to the sub-tropical suburban spot where I lived as if, somehow, for my own sake. I never returned the call.

In spite of such foolishness we all became close friends, an association in which Ulla's personality at once showed up clear and positive. Ulla was born in Copenhagen in 1905. The only child of a successful Danish physician, she grew up in luxury, yet she had a genuine love for the common soil and for the gentlemanly labors of country living. The advantages of birth never obstructed the earthy radiance of Ulla's human spectrum. Her social being and behavior were endlessly versatile. When Kay said, "I married the good earth", he spoke fondly but inadequately, for he also married the drawing room, the best rose Canton, the sad clown and many surprises. She was a short and dynamic figure, rather broad, not revealing much bosom or hip, but whole, elastic and quick to move. Quick to embrace, quick to stab with a lance of wit or sarcasm (often in French), quick to annihilate — once or twice myself — since sweetness or stupidity were targets that must naturally be hit square in the middle; and quick to help when help was needed. A shadow of helplessness stealing across the face of a friend was an inspiring sight to Ulla. Her features were even but not striking enough to describe, and she was beautiful. She had fine skin and a shapely skull, and the expression seen on Etruscan heads or the small clay faces from Vera Cruz in Mexico, the same archaic wisdom and amusement being common to all three.

Kay Nielsen was born in Copenhagen in 1886. His parents had both been illustrious theater people. "They brought me up in a tense atmosphere of art," he said. His father, Professor Martinius Nielsen, was an actor and the manager of the Dagmartheater, and his mother Oda a loved singer and star of the Royal Theater in Copenhagen. Their son was a man whose tall, impeccable manners caused an occasional courteous stoop. Ordinarily he wore a tweed jacket, the pockets full of cigarettes for which he was always groping. In other respects he seemed to resemble that Lohan of the Buddhistic discipleship who was represented in the company of a tame crane and an adoring deer. He has been likened to St. Francis, but I prefer the Lohan, of whom I have an old painting which by a strange chance looks enough like Kay Nielsen to have been his Asiatic brother. Kay all his life had an affinity for the Oriental. He was a very talented man yet he was so free of opinions that he left none behind for any portrait by quotation. His work must speak instead. Intellectually he did not have strong identifications but in his feelings he had empathy for many aspects of man and nature. Asked today what they recall most about him people invariably answer, "He never said an unkind work about anybody."

To live near Kay and Ulla was to be acutely aware of them. They changed our lives as life went around and around. Their lives touched ours, touched, grazed and left a mark, a groove, and in it the needle of my memory goes around and around. For me the sound it makes is elegy, harmonious, melancholy or funny. Elegy has many minds and it is serviceable, for in elegy is the habit of memory that conserves minor things as if they were the most significant. This elegy in memory of Kay and Ulla Nielsen is not an epitaph. I hope that the facts are reliable for the purpose.

Kay and Ulla Nielsen came into our lives foreign, even cryptic, yet speaking English with ease, and in Ulla's case with a pleased curiosity to learn the tang of native expressions and endearments. Our local affections seized them greedily.

As a young reader I had preposterously supposed that the artist had lived in the country he painted, a country of rare decorative landscape, or in the vicinity of the stars, which must be close to his home. Unexpectedly meeting Kay Nielsen I had a hard time to get rid of the feeling that he still belonged a great way off, a long way beyond these suburbs. Even a time of war and alarm did not seem to draw his guarded sensibilities into its snare although he was, when I first knew him, acting as "block warden" when the siren blew at night. He patrolled the streets to make certain that no lights were visible, and handed out expensive gas masks, all part of the military game that residents of the suburbs were asked to play and which some of them played so seriously. Kay did as he was asked, but remained uninvolved. As I came to know him he appeared to be the model for his tall heroes, and like them seemed puritanic, as much monk as painter, never quite coming out of the hieratic forest.

Stirred and bewildered by the luck that had made me the neighbor of Kay Nielsen I turned back to the book that had left its mark on my childhood, hoping to step again into the obsessive world he had given me, hoping to be able to find a name for whatever it had been that had gripped me, rising from these pages. I had been a believing young person and now I was an unbelieving woman, yet it was not a faith in anything with a mere tag like magic that I had grown out of, for that had never meant more than entertainment, the tune that turned the lock to let the story in and out. And magic, in any case, was only the expected melody, and not the real amazement, the intense music, the long clear tone straight from the instrument of art itself. This hypnotic sound I had known, as the paintings fulfilled the stories, and it had become a part of me and my memory, but how to define it? I opened the book, carefully and hopefully. There they were! Those people with elongated bodies, slim, majestic and with high shoulders supporting faces of diffident haughtiness. Had I been fascinated by alien character and person? Was I in love with lordly profiles? Caught by the appeal of spectral innocence, of exquisite and fateful landscapes? Had I, young and impressionable, created some of this myself, for myself? I looked and looked, much as I used to, years ago, but now with purpose added. Gradually I understood that what had moved me most had been the commandment of the artist's emotion coming vividly from his mind in the occult movement of style across the page. Now I was older and I could recognize the excitement of a first-rate imagination and the skills of design that belonged with it, and I saw them as consolation for the loss of more naive and younger enjoyments, and as consolation even for the passing and unreturning years. Fondly, respectfully, I turned the pages of the book, and they fell open to the mounted knight, one large hand holding the bridle and the other hand holding the slender girl before him on the horse. Once more, I could feel the size, the weight, the heat of that hand. And I never brought myself to tell my feelings to Kay.

It did not require a long acquaintance to reveal that Ulla's love for her husband was the emotional and practical apparatus that ran their lives. To love a man as she did was not only utter devotion but an enterprise to which she gave inventive attention. Hyperbole is required to say that her concern was that of a shepherd over his flock, for Kay, the calmest and best-collected of sheep could appear, in the focus of anxiety, to become many sheep, each of whom she knew to be sick, cold, wet and pursued by a coyote. A fine pack of perils. And hard work. But she was no fool, certainly not. She never permitted his image to look mothered or badgered. If she did badger him it was a process so original, so loving, so blamelessly provoking as to be a work of true finesse.

Kay Nielsen had come to California in 1936 at the invitation of the Festival Association of the Hollywood Bowl to do the scenic production for Max Reinhardt's "Everyman". He remained to work for Walt Disney, designing the aetherial "Bald Mountain" sequence for "Fantasia". When the second war broke over Europe he sent for Ulla who had stayed in Denmark. She eventually obtained passage on the Gripsholm, and brought with her the two Scotties and her best silver, and was given to recalling that her mother had protested, "I know you must go to Kay, but why don't you leave your silver here? Your boat might be sunk by submarines." It was the truth that Ulla must come to Kay, who was surrounded by the most attractive women in Hollywood. Kay drew women as a tall tree draws lightning.

With Ulla's arrival on the coast the Nielsens set up their household in the good style to which they had been accustomed at home. However, the connection with Disney was gradually severed, and the little house around the corner from us to which they had withdrawn was, we rightly assumed, a necessary step down for them in the way of living. What their former style had been became apparent as they transformed a cottage with charm that suggested they had always lived well and could still show how it was done, even very modestly. They had acquired in Hollywood, at an auction, some Chinese furniture, including a red lacquered table and some teak wood chairs. A fair nucleus. From her big home the playwright, Zoe Akins, who had become a close friend, supplied a tapestry wall-hanging, a carved chest on legs, and a portrait, an American primitive of a mystical child, behind her a wandering river, perhaps the far-away Wabash and two carefully located trees. Also, and important, she gave them a soft chair for Kay especially to rest in. There was a painted Chinese fan that had belonged to Kay's mother. It hung on one wall in a fan-shaped box. So then they had a tiny drawing-room and the few things it contained were all desirable. But one thing they had that my husband and I did not admire was a carving by Gauguin, a round thick polished cross-piece of cherry-wood, an early work of romantic character, the head of a dull, virtuous woman. One could tell. It also had belonged to Kay's mother who, the Nielsens said, had befriended Madame Gauguin in Denmark when the artist deserted his family.

One recalls their environment in detail because it seemed to indicate the growing difference in their lives between what they had been accustomed to and a new set of facts. In Denmark they had lived in an aura of two generations of theater, art and the lights of family prominence. Now they lived chiefly with memories, the illumination of the past. Domestically it had been a correct and pleasant existence. "In winter it was night most of the day," Ulla told us, "and the house-boy — he was from Java — toward evening would come into the drawing room and turn on more lights and bring us our drinks. Then he would prepare the dinner." At this point she sighed, remembering that the dishes from breakfast and luncheon lay unwashed in her sink. "And in summer when we gave an evening party we would make it beautiful for the company. We borrowed the night blooming Cereus from the botanical garden. Ah, it was all excellent, and with music." But how well she could pretend that everything was 'oughkeigh'. (I told her that was the way it was spelled.) To dine there was an occasion, never merely a meal. Fabulous ries taffel, lace tablecloth, candles and the silver that did not sink in the North Sea. "Ulla, where did you learn to cook?" "I made my living as a cateress, you know." This was a lie, told for parties and especially for Americans. As a lady who had never worked for her living she would once in a while break down and work to clean her own house, but just as often, as a lady, she ignored the dirt as an element of life beneath her notice, and when guests were coming to dinner I have heard her say haughtily, "When I see the whites of their eyes I start to get ready."

People were drawn to them and people delighted to do things for them, not in a spirit of charity but because the donor relished being that much closer to them. One friend gave them an automobile, a practical used Austin, just right for the two of them and the dogs. Their next door neighbor, Erma Jacobsen, looked after them and worried about them "as much as I did about my own family." And eventually the elderly man from whom they were buying their cottage came to them and said, "I'm not going to live much longer, I'm a sick man, you know. My son is heartless, and when you don't pay your installments he'll throw you out. Now, let's fix the deed."

It is not likely that they guessed how they struck their American friends. Although so different, so distinguishable in personality, they seemed a single involved being. They were two people and they were one self. An amazement to Americans, ardent and devoted though we may be, rarely prepared to understand the meaning of union.

The connection with the Disney Studios had been suspended initially as a leave of absence but became permanent when plans for "The Little Mermaid" on which Kay was working were given up. It was rumored that he was not well pleased to see his designs altered during the process of animation. In any case Kay was out of a job.

"Job" is the wrong word for the fastidious and imaginative tone of his work, but it is the right word for bread, shoes and gasoline. Could he, perhaps, teach at one of the art schools in Los Angeles? Ulla began to make faces. At this she was petrifying. She managed to show all of her teeth at once and then, returning to normal, usually made some pompous remark — on this occasion, "Oh deah, how the cause of puah art would suffah!" She claimed that all the students, men as well as women, would fall in love with Kay. Kay, starting to protest, got into one of his bad fits of coughing. By the time he came out of it Ulla had decided to raise chickens, and he agreed at once.

Their friend, the Danish pianist and entertainer Victor Borge, had a profitable business in rearing and selling Cornish game chickens. Along with creatures in general, the Nielsens had a true heart for chickens. They understood, even liked the silly ways of chickens, knew how to talk to them, and had a sentimental memory of the many chickens they had kept at their country home in Denmark. Soon, going into their house one might hear the soft sleepy cheeping of baby chicks in the small kitchen, cosy in their baskets or in incubators made by Kay. It was a pleasant greeting but an unsettling one to catch these barnyard voices only a few feet away while one stood uncertainly in the proprieties of the drawing room. And finally and somehow, and in spite of many preparations and much work, the enterprise Cornish Game Hen came to nothing. So, characteristically, the chickens became a gesture of graciousness and generosity, and I got the last Cornish game hen as a gift when one morning I heard the gate open and saw Ulla standing outside with a small wagon she had borrowed from her young neighbor, Peter. Elevated on the little squeaky vehicle lay a Cornish hen wrapped in shining cellophane. On her breast quivered an enormous red bow saved from Christmas. Ulla, walking solemnly, pulled this elegant freight down the path and presented it to me with a fine show of manners. She might have been delivering Cleopatra on a barge.

It was not easy to see why an artist of Kay's reputation should find his abilities asking for employment. Yet it was easy to see that his disadvantage lay in the narrowness of his range in a day that was suspicious of fantasy — unless neurotic or Joycean — that "the Golden Age of Illustration" in which his name had been notable along with those of Morris, Beardsley, Boecklin, Pyle, Rackham, Dulac and their brotherhood had closed, and however vital his skill in decoration he had no ease in self-promotion. Only an occasional haughtiness. Both war and competition are hard on the arts and crafts as on other decencies. In other times his talent and reputation might have carried him without anxiety for the rest of his life, yet already in the forties of the century and his own middle-fifties his successes, both European and American, were all in the past and apparently out of sight, and he was living obscurely in a mortgaged cottage in the foothill suburbs, and no prospects ahead. Apprehension about money became chronic, and also there was the crucial matter of ill-health. In spite of his tall appearance of well-being, Kay was not strong and Ulla,

since no one dares be sick without plenty of cash, did not mention the fact that she was threatened with diabetes.

Unexpectedly, and while they were bravely and foolishly trying to cast themselves for help on the tender breasts of small fowl, they received a call from a stranger who was to make a great difference in their lives.

Miss Jasmine Britton was the Supervising Librarian of the Los Angeles school system. Being a specialist in books for young readers Kay Nielsen was known to her. Coming into his home for the first time and hearing baby chickens in the next room Miss Britton, in addition to being astonished, soon discovered that the chickens were an emergency of Kay's idleness. She held another position which was to be of use to him. She was on the board of the Filippa Pollia Foundation established by Dr. Joseph A. Pollia in memory of his young daughter. The purpose of the Foundation was to dispense the funds originally intended for the child's education, and in ways that would offer pleasure in the arts, and cultural advantages to other children. Miss Britton was involved in finding the best ways for spending the Foundation's money. She secured, as a gift to the City of Los Angeles from the Pollia Foundation, a commission for Kay Nielsen to paint a mural in the library of the Central Junior High School where the student body was multi-racial and came from homes in the modest and low-income brackets. This commission, and the painting of the mural which began in 1942, rescued the Nielsens from their immediate worries.

It was the first mural that Kay had painted although his experience of large-scale stage decoration was related. But a new technique of applying design and the enlarging of the basic cartoon had to be learned with camera and magic lantern for a painting thirty-four feet long by nineteen high. For the young half-Americans of the school Kay painted a mural called "The First Spring", a generously expanded version of Genesis I: 25: "And God made the beast of the earth after his kind, and cattle after their kind, and everything that creepeth on the earth after his kind; and God saw that it was good." Kay also saw to it that his own version was good, improving on the brief list of the Creator with a gathering of lyrical zoology. The tender herds are shepherded by the Archangel Gabriel riding on very tall cattle, there is a stir of birds and dashing streams and a host of creatures of jungle, savannah and ocean stroll or float through the first softly bright unpolluted environment. God had not specified floral details but Ulla filled them in, after her kind, groups of sessile bunched violets, potentillas and campanulas. Somehow an unscriptural ladybug got into this early Paradise and a monkey holds a pet parakeet on his wrist. The animals all seem to be congratulating themselves on having escaped the long bloody tedium of evolution and, a very local touch, the valley quail of California, quite as in Kay's own neighborhood, hang about discretely, as their custom is.

"We built a moving platform for Kay to reach the top", Miss Britton recalls. "It took him much longer than we expected. He was not well and he smoked continually. I had a problem in war times to find a carton of cigarettes a week." It finally required three years of measuring, climbing, painting, smoking and coughing to finish the mural. "We paid Kay every two weeks $200." Ulla, besides adding a few delights God had omitted, made friends among the students.

The presentation of the mural was an event attended by the educational and social elite. Arthur Millier, art critic of the *Los Angeles Times*, reviewed the evening prominently and praised the mural as "one of the most beautiful wall paintings in America." The work was accepted by the Board of Education of Los Angeles to selections from Haydn's Oratorio "The Creation" provided by the school glee club and orchestra. "The mural has so impressed Los Angeles educators", continued Millier, "that the artist is already at work on sketches for a mural project in another high school here."

As a multi-racial, educational and social experiment serving a community of many backgrounds, the Central High School had been considered an important development of the city school system. Without warning, it was announced by the Board of Education that the building was needed for administration headquarters, being located as it was, close to the civic and administrative center of the City of Los Angeles itself. One year after the mural was finished, publicly accepted and acclaimed, the school was closed. The commodious library graced by the painting was coveted by the Board for the official meeting room and Kay Nielsen's mural was stripped from the wall. The library became a practical business office with charts of urban school districts for decor.

Miss Britton caught up with the crime. Today she recalls laconically, "I raged." Appearing before the Board, and not so laconically, she threatened to reveal the details to the *Los Angeles Times*, pointing out the pleasure and care with which the *Times* would explore every aspect of what could become a first-rate political scandal. The mural had been the gift to the City of Los Angeles from a distinguished naturalized Italian-American physician, and painted by an artist with a reputation on two continents and in England. The Board, elected by trusting citizens and paid by their taxes, a body of men who had campaigned as the best procurable for the public responsibility of providing education and ideals to the city's children, these were the men who had committed the unbelievable vulgarity of tearing from the library walls one of America's most beautiful murals. Not to mention the expense of wasted money and years of time and talent. The shaken politicians, gazing at the hard-hitting and articulate menace addressing them, quickly saw their peril and offered to pay for transferring the mural to another high school. But there was no school with a library wall — or any wall — large enough to accommodate the mural. Fortunately Sutter Junior High in the San Fernando Valley of Los Angeles was in the process of being built. Plans were changed to accommodate the mural, but installed in its new home it was all too clear that much of it had been totally destroyed by faulty removal and storage. Too shocked to contemplate the ruin, Kay at first refused to work on it. Eventually he was persuaded to do so, however. Characteristically he drove himself mercilessly, often working ten hours

and more a day, starting high up on the scaffolding in the cool of the morning and gradually descending to work at lower levels as the heat built up near the ceiling. Ulla and a decorator, Einar Petersen, worked with him. The entire restoration took two years and unquestionably was a drain on Kay's health. The sickening blow to Kay's pride and sensibilities was a matter his shocked friends avoided probing. The second mural, mentioned by critic Millier, and perhaps promoted by the Board to placate a watchful Miss Britton, got under way in 1946. It was not paid for by the school system, however, but by little monies of student funds and the P.T.A. "The Canticle of the Sun", (first called "Salutation to the Dawn"), is in Emerson Junior High School, a school used in the teacher training program of the University of California at Westwood in Los Angeles. This painting has the same decorative and lyrical appeal that filled the squarefootage of the first. High in the center the sun, a strong white figure naked save for a hyacinthine scarf, but obviously male, strides across the sky above the landscape, his step immense and bold and his arms extended, held out in transparencies of early illumination. A horizontal sweep of gold hair, one of Kay's pictorial devices, adds to the effect of speed. On either side there is a world of wakening flocks and shepherds and plowmen in the fields. There is a terraced hill crowded with houses and porticoes and holding a church at the top, and below it an inlet of water with a sailing caravel shaped like a huge walnut shell. Here and there are signs of work in the midst of unbroken serenity. It is difficult to transfer to words the calm of the landscape where just enough people are laboring to avoid making it a busy place. Every contour of hill and field had been foreseen, it appears, a long time ago and lay waiting in patient tranquility for the artist to come from the north. And what, in a semi-tropic place, was he remembering or dreaming? For off in a strange distance there rises a magnificent, many-spired pinnacle of snow. Exquisiteness, grandeur and tenderness inevitably come to mind as one looks at this painting. It takes courage in our times to be so angelic.

Then, his good fortune still holding, Kay executed for the Wong Chapel in the First Congregational Church of Los Angeles an altar painting based on the Twenty-Third Psalm. Here the shepherd of the poem climbs in a gigantic stretch up a jagged rock ascent holding one foolish lamb in his arms while other sheep are perched in a dangerous meadow overhead. The familiar theme of comforting Biblical promise is situated in an unfamiliar setting of bold angularity made by the shepherd's long legs and the jutting rocks. It is not the usual consoling pastoral. As if to assuage the surprise of the orthodox worshipper there is one of this artist's mysterious telescopic distances where a flock of sheep rest like clovering proverbs in green pastures.

Kay Nielsen, being an illustrator, worked from a literary imagination. With extraordinary richness of detail, refinement and ephemeral delicacy he transformed the matter of other mens' minds into his own kind of deliberate charm. He achieved personal style by slow, attentive, monkish reliance on insight into the decorator's means of giving pleasure. Though naturally conversant with the historic advance of painting in the twentieth century he remained aloof from the times in his work. Excelling in the lyrical and the poetical was the ideal that absorbed him and he made no effort to modernize the subject-matter that had governed his style. He had, perhaps as an inheritance from parents of the theater, a good stage sense of how to cross a page or stand still off center. In his early work under the shadow of Beardsley he was elegantly morbid or perverse, a thing he could manage by the droop of an eyelid or the turn of a silk ankle, and in his later work the morbidity was gone while the tension sometimes remained as an element of manner — that slight pull away from the representational, an attractive awkwardness or distortion of common forms. The unspoiled manners he practiced in social relationships were the same manners he practiced in art, special to his own person and never ambivalent. The murals in the schools contain nothing controversial, either aesthetic or social, at a time when proletarian sympathies were easily suggested by just an extra breadth to the shoulders, an added stoop to the back. They contain neither belief nor unbelief, although possibly an old fashioned trust in the civilizing powers of beauty, and that, if implied was not meant to be insisted on. His paintings could not have been moralistic. They were, in a modestly aristocratic way, utilitarian, in the sense that it is a pleasure to use anything made to be seen. The murals were made to give pleasure.

With the completion of the Wong Chapel painting in 1947 Kay was again out of work and again there were no prospects of any kind in sight. The blank wall they had stared at before was once more coldly staring back at them. They groaned, and their groans were gallant. No one had to pity them. Their friends brought them unnecessary luxuries — exotic hors d'oeuvres and caviar — gifts that would not vulgarly suggest they needed sensible food.

It was to be six years before Kay again received a commission. This they could not have known. However, their nervousness about their affairs drove them into a kind of boredom in which Ulla herself seized upon any activity. Her sensitive slim hands were therapeutic, or so she said, and anyone who complained of a stiff neck was quickly gathered in by her and renovated.

Because of their problems their thoughts often turned back to Denmark. Especially as Christmas drew near nostalgia came with it. They prepared as they would at home. Ulla baked some very large hard cookies, indestructible ginger-bread slabs they were, large enough to decorate with angels, birds and flowers in graceful lines of colored sugar-icing. Each cookie was put in a box made by her, and the box covered with dark blue paper printed with gold stars. The cookie was displayed through clear cellophane and one stared at it and applauded it and never dreamed of eating that much magnificence which, in any case, was hard enough to crack every tooth in one's head. One of the loveliest things that appeared in their cottage at Christmas was the strings of small white angels Ulla cut from waste paper and hung across windows and doorways, or nestled in greenery. Separate angels, always white paper, were also on

the Christmas tree, the only ornament I remember. For the tree they might have to make an extended search through the markets until they found one most like the conifer they used in Denmark. The one I recollect was a handsome white fir, a noble small tree of proud bearing, its topmost tip right against the low ceiling. They loved it, and paid much more for it than they would have for more ordinary trees. "Twelve dollars," said Ulla happily, "only twelve dollars to take us home on Christmas Eve." And she hung white angels all over it and put white tapers generously among the branches in holders.

The night I went over to see the tree I walked through a savage wind storm, for a Santa Ana had hit our part of the county. I got into the house quickly to shut out the commotion of the wind and stood praising the tree, beautiful in its simple white decoration. "But surely in all this wind you won't light it?" "Why not?" they asked together. "Because if it caught fire your house and everything for miles around would go up in a blaze. There would be no stopping it in this wind." "So," said Ulla, "in south California the wind is blowing, and in Denmark we light the tapers." "Naturally we light the tapers," said Kay. I protested, "You know all about icebergs and polar bears, but you don't know anything about chapparal fires." "Nothing will happen," said Ulla, "Just watch. It will be lovely." "Light the tapers, Ulla," said Kay eagerly. Ulla was already reaching for a box of wooden matches and gradually the tree was illuminated with softly glowing buds of peril. It gave off a silver light and in the warmth of it the little angels began to twirl slowly. It could not have been lovelier. It could not have been more dangerous. As the wind continued to roar and shake the house I saw that Kay and Ulla were gazing at their tree in quiet contentment. They said nothing. They were far away, they were scarcely, except for their eyes, in their bodies at all. They were at home in a dark and snowy country sitting in their drawing room in the shine and silver of their favorite Christmas tree.

Suddenly it happened. A branch of resinous fir ignited. Ulla sprang to her feet and her right arm struck out, quick and accurate as a snake. The fire was put out, the candle adjusted and re-lit. She gave me a look. Once again they were translated, floating in gentle brightness, floating home. They had arrived. Now if I would depart, the house-boy from Java would come into the room and bring with him on a tray a hot and spirited drink and they could toast the little angels that twirled among the fir branches. I left as carefully as I could, and I knew they were not aware of me going out into the wind, the wind of the foothills that was always so frightening, beating on dwellings, shaking the windows and tearing at steeples and gardens. As I walked home, buffeted by the storm, I kept the image of the lighted fir tree in my mind where it stood, serene and safe, neither blown out nor on fire.

With money worries acute the Nielsens decided to sell something, choosing a large, bronze vase of Oriental origin, bought as part of a "parcel" at auction. Unfortunately it turned out to be a fake.

But there existed something in their house that we had

never yet seen. As they, or rather Ulla, pulled a heavy wooden box out of a closet we had no idea what it contained. They opened the box, lifting three metal hasps, and with a stir of tissue paper and other wrappings, revealed its contents. There were nineteen remarkable gouache illustrations of ample miniature size, thirteen inches square including borders, for "A Thousand and One Nights" on which Kay had worked from 1918 to 1922. His designs were made to accompany a translation from the original Arabic by Professor Arthur Christensen. Intended for Danish publication the printing of the work in Denmark had been given up because of high costs after the war, and although simultaneous publication had been arranged for Paris, London and New York, all plans eventually fell through because of difficulties over the translations.

Early Italy, Persia, India and China were influences freely acknowledged by Kay Nielsen in what he called his "artistic wandering", and these came clearly to view in the rich paintings being slowly removed from the large box. To the old stories told by the heroic and calculating Scheherazade, Kay gave fresh reasons for their perpetuation, presenting each crucial, chosen drama of her recital with visible drama of his own skill, adding faces of doom or desire, setting the motions of ballet turning around the fates of lovers and fools, schemers, enchanters, princes and slaves. Here he was happy, even among cruelties and injustice. This was the world he liked to inhabit, where fantasy needed no apology and was as real as bricks and stones, a world in which his imagination was free to live in the midst of an exotic classic, a realm where things naturally demanded a transcendent array of astounding variety, where all human means of life — houses, walls, clothes, furnishings, break into art and ornament like pods that split from weight of seed. Therefore draperies, costumes, architecture, floral indulgence and strong delicate traceries. Therefore the intense contrivance of pattern both in color and in the black and white of the amazing text borders until it all seemed, in an odd way hard to assess, to be a part of the contrivance and even the drive or desperation of the tales. Decoration held more than its own ends. While by the artist's discipline the miniatures escaped congestion yet for the beholder there was no limit to the absorption of looking. Only by the mercy of fatigue was one saved from the endless differences, the exhilaration of variety, especially of the borders both black and white as well as colored, which could not be quite believed, only accepted. It was in one of the latter that I caught sight of a foreign detail, a pair of knitting needles, busy with the heel of a green sock from which the strand of wool floated as the stem of a flowering vine, and in the corner of the same border there appeared a surely non-Arabian head-covering, an Alpine hat with pheasant feathers, not likely ever hung on a hatrack in the Sultan's palace. Mystery and amusement lie in these unordained objects. No one will ever know how their intrusive delights stole with a breath of snow into hot Arabia. And there was yet more to take one's attention. Kay was given to pillars, some fluted, some spiralling, some like evanescent vertebrae cleansed of flesh and seeming spiritual. Scheherazade's talent for sensual arousement was discretely matched by Kay's celery-white bodies of naked girls and the ivory plums of their small breasts.

The question to consider was — could these twenty elaborate watercolors be turned into a lot of plain money? There were actually twenty-one, but one was missing. It was the property of the Art Institute of Chicago, purchased as a prize at the Institute's International Watercolor Exhibition of 1925. Only twice the series had been shown. The few hundreds of dollars of the prize money was the total that the artist had received for his hard and talented labors. Now, at my husband's suggestion, he offered them to *Life*, the magazine that had been reproducing in color the famous paintings of European galleries. Kay's work was turned down. The illustrations for "A Thousand and One Nights" remained in the heavy wooden box where they were kept.

As the forties closed their world continued to fall away. It had once been a very good world but what remained was chiefly a frame of memories. They could pose there, but it was sad. They could still be proud of name and talent, but talent had no work to do. They could still, in garments grown familiar, enter a room and compliment the company by being there. So few people know how to enter a room with unpremeditated manners. So few people know how just to be present. Fewer still can make a living at it.

At length anxiety and hope together took them home to Denmark. It was not a simple departure. One Scottie remained from the pair and he went with them, also a cat in a basket, and just before sailing their cabin was so crowded with things brought along for Kay's comfort that he had no room to lie down. Their arrival in Denmark was a new and lonely experience. There were no reporters nor photographers to meet them. Once, with the two smart dogs on the double leash, they had been favorites with the press. Along with Kay's parents they had been a conspicuous family. This was no longer the case. Absence and the second war and political and social changes had broken the continuity. And soon Kay found it impossible to mend the break with his former reputation even in his own country. Styles and preferences in art were in new hands. A Christmas card from Ulla in 1950 ran:

Dear Friends!!! Another Xmas and we are still stuck in little wet old Denmark. You never saw so much rain and it is blowing a gail (sic). Of course this little place may get too hot for comfort all of a sudden (a political reference?) and all the things we now feel we have to put in order may not be worth it . . . We are still striving to get going but there is something funny, the more we strive the deeper we sink into a cold grey porridge . . . But, children this is meant to be a Xmas greeting . . . Love to you . . . from Pinky, Kay and Ulla. (Pinky was the cat.)

In 1952 the Christmas card came from around the corner. They had returned to us but again America failed them and they tried Denmark once more, spending frigid winter months at their country home in Bakkebolle, Nyraad. Of this place we had heard when we first knew them — roses, fruits, vegetables, green lawns, a small hill for the house to stand on, and the sea for excursions "when we were sailing in our little old boat called the Flatfish." "We are peasants," Kay had said frequently and fervently when they spoke of Bakkebolle and we knew they loved it. Particularly when Ulla said, "Anyone taking away from me one square foot of earth that is mine I shall be happy to slit the throat of." But they lost it, perhaps to indebtedness, we never knew. After their last return to southern California Kay described the final sojourn in Denmark. "I sat all day in blankets inside a cloud of my freezing breath." The hardships of their visit left him coughing more and with less energy.

Now that they had returned, that valiant structure, Ulla's love for Kay, was again in full sight, the articulated energy and passionate worry that held together at all points and operated under any stress. Ulla's love brought images of speech to mind while Kay's was a quiet and gallant kind of dependence, and no one gave it names. It had, from the first, been understood by their friends that when it came to one of them to die the other would follow soon. There seemed nothing morbid in their hopes. Other people might have to face loneliness and desolation as widows or widowers but fate could not be so crude to Kay and Ulla Nielsen. There must be reserved for them something more courteous, an acknowledgment by death of a memorable relationship, a simultaneous and accommodating departure, or at least an easy arrangement for the survivor not to survive. Kay only extracted from Ulla the promise to wait for six months. But life itself had still one solution to their difficulties in store, and our own country once again had more to offer the artist than his indifferent homeland. After the long barren seasons of nothing at all there came an unexpected autumn of harvest.

People who quietly do the kindest things are apt to be people who want nothing said about their deeds. Deeds, however, are history, and most of history is big, gross and deplorable. Any scrap of it that is decent ought to be set down. The truth is that there exists a second Britton sister, Helen Britton Holland, who, although she lives on the north coast had developed a keen devotion to Kay's two murals in the south. Hearing about the cold grey porridge in which they had been stuck on both trips to Denmark she sent the Nielsens fifteen hundred dollars as first payment on a third wall painting, this one to be commissioned for Whitman College in Walla Walla, Washington, which she had attended in her early college years. That money being spent before they got out of the porridge and back to California she sent another similar amount and Kay was engaged to paint a mural of about one-third the size of those in southern California.

It was possibly a surprise (as well as a disappointment) to the donor, who had in mind the visual pleasures of the first murals, that Kay selected as his theme a tragic pioneer episode from the history of the Whitman family for whom the college is a memorial — missionaries and pioneer bene-factors of the local Indians and their victims by massacre. He could have found endless reasons for contented or excited painting of his kind had he wandered through the rain forests, those aisles of damp green, of black trees and swinging moss, where the fauna, large and small, would easily step onto his canvas from ferns and sorrel. He made the sterner choice — the fates of Narcissa and Marcus Whitman. Beneath coral-like branches and heavy foliage a semi-circle of mourners stand about a dead body. Behind them rises the cone of a teepee. The scene gives way to an immense buttress of light, as in the other murals, holding in its transparency a pale stockade and a fenced grave, and at the bottom a felicity of flowers and grasses. Lifting far up in the future of clouds and mists are the dome and pillars of the state, the occupancy of law and order. Across the plains in the upper centre comes a long procession of ghostly Conestoga or prairie schooners, their white tops mincing forward like shells from the liquid distance which is also the desert of thirst and migration, while the eyes of the viewer return to the pale, haunting medallion of the death-scene down there in the woods. In his final work Kay Nielsen did not use fantasy nor the drama of exotic legend. He used the drama of human life and its chances of safe arrival or disaster.

The mural had actually not been painted in the north but in southern California in San Marino at the home of a friend who offered adequate wall-space and light, neither of which existed in the cottage where only the early stages could be accomplished. While it was being finished Ulla invited me to see the progress of the painting and also for a special observance. In her childhood in Denmark, she said, she was often invited to a birthday party and it was traditional to serve an exceedingly rich mixture of vanilla ice-cream and chocolate. "It was heavenly. It always made me sick as a cat. I was forbidden to eat it and when I came home from a party and spit up, my mother would know I had disobeyed, and I would be whipped." We went together in the little Austin to buy the ice-cream. It was a very hot day in June. We hurried, concerned as to how well, if at all, the ice-cream would stand up in the weather. We were on Blanche Street, and as we approached an intersection we saw traffic halted and blocking the way ahead. "What's going on in Blonsh Street?" enquired Ulla with an irritated French emphasis, and since we could not turn around we walked ahead to investigate the jam. A considerable crowd stood about the intersection. Two cars had collided. Their drivers, two very angry men, were fighting savagely in the middle of the street. People stood about, either disgusted or entertained by the spectacle, whistling and shouting encouragement. Ulla snorted and I could see that she was, without preliminaries, getting into a good rage. Now she strutted into the street right toward the fighting men. A few people made gestures as if to pull her back. She brushed them off and drew a deep breath. Ulla never wasted profanity. She hoarded it for a righteous cause. Certainly, while the expensive ice-cream sat melting in the high temperature, she had one at this moment. "Gentlemen, Goddamn it," she shouted to the antagonists, "Stop your fighting!" The men relaxed their holds and for a few seconds left off hitting each other as they stared at her in amazement. "It's hot as hell," she continued with increased power, "And my ice-cream is melting!" The crowd broke into laughter and cheers. The fighters slowly and reluctantly fell apart and after a threatening gesture or two shuffled back to their cars, muttering and red-faced. As the crowd stood admiring Ulla a bystander approached her, bowed, and said, "Lady, what do you do when you aren't stopping fights?" "Why didn't you stop them yourself?" she snapped. "Me, lady? They would have killed me." Ulla began to breathe more evenly, and she made a queenly gesture towards me backward over her shoulder. "My friend is having a birthday." The connection was clear — ice-cream, birthday — and everyone smiled and drew aside, and as the intersection cleared we sped off while I clutched a vanilla puddle in my lap and waved through the dusty windshield of the little Austin.

While we ate our chocolate and ice-cream, an extraordinary voluptuous bog into which we waded with happy sighs, I rehearsed for Kay the Battle of Blonsh. "Ulla always wins," he murmured appreciatively. "Well, of course", Ulla responded, "Because when I was born my father refused to look at me for two days, since I was not a boy, and I have had to spend my life trying to prove that I am as good as one. "Thank God you're not a boy," said Kay, "what would become of me?" and he tried to laugh, but as it often did, a laugh made him cough. Ulla sat watching him, and I, too, could see what she saw and continued to look at with pleading sadness, as if to coax from his face a greyness of the living flesh which seemed to proclaim what neither of them, by speech or silence, could bear to admit. Several days later she startled me by saying, "He won't die before he finishes it." That was the moment to enquire, "What ails Kay?", but I could not quite ask it. She never gave it a name. Perhaps from superstition. Don't give it a name.

She was right, he finished it, and they delivered the mural to Whitman College at Walla Walla. But not without ordeal. Returning to southern California they took Route One late at night in the middle stage of their journey. It was a lonely road, a narrow cliff road, one that many preople avoid, day or night. At some point in the darkness it became apparent that they were being followed by the only other car in sight. Wherever there was straightaway room to pass Ulla gave the other car the opportunity to do so, but the driver kept ominously in her tracks until finally he swerved ahead and stopped directly in front of the Austin. All around them was the solitary black night, and below them the cliff and steep rocks, and down there somewhere the Pacific Ocean, twice as near for being invisible. Suddenly Ulla, as much from nervous frenzy as from good sense, put her foot down hard on the gas pedal and shot past the other car, barely escaping between it and the cliff in the awful margin that remained. There was nothing else she could do, she explained afterwards. "I had to save Kay." In her lights she had seen the dark figure of a man getting out of the other car and he held something in his hand. "Was Kay frightened?" I enquired. "Fast asleep, thank God."

Over the years the two Scotties had both died, and presently a distraction that gave them comfort but added expense, was a new dog. If *new* was an epithet that could be applied to an animal that looked, at least to me, as worn and down in the shanks as an old scrub brush. I must have been

genuinely wrong for Kay and Ulla insisted he — a French poodle — had the most irreproachable good breeding. At this I laughed rudely, yet I could see that Kay himself and the poodle had a peculiar regard for each other. The dog would sit by Kay's chair and stare at him with love — stare and stare — until Kay, almost embarrassed would say gently, "That's enough, now, my dear," and Ulla would take the poodle for a walk. Or just a for talk. Her method of conversing with the dog was to hold him by the nose and address him, her head close to his, in the Danish language enhanced and softened by her rolling, sweetening tongue. The poodle would be spell-bound. She was telling him funny stories about other dogs. I forget his name. I called him "The Little Old Man".

Repeatedly Ulla said, "I can't work at anything, I can't do anything unless Kay praises it. He has to say it is beautiful." And when the weather was benign he would sit in a chair in the garden, and she would dig a little or grub at a plant near his foot, looking up and joking. He would nod and smile. I found them one afternoon when she was twining a branch of grapevine into the back fence. "That could be one of the vines left over from the old vineyards in these foothills years ago," I said. She finished her job with a strand of raffia, and we both looked at Kay. "Beautiful," he said softly. Then as we stood in silence, looking at him in anxiety, he roused himself to speak again. "Beautiful, beautiful." It became more evident as the time passed that Kay was weaker and showed no signs of regaining energy. He could tolerate almost no food. He would sit all day in his chair, dozing, coughing, or he would spend the days in bed. Yet it was easier for him to breathe sitting up in his chair, held together in shreds of life and still struggling in correctness, gentleness and courtesy against the disarray that was crushing him down. It is a very mean thing to watch from glimpse to glimpse how death approaches, how, like a long black train winding through bare foothills and ravines it shows itself first at a distance, and then near and more near, until the dismal slow fiend is suddenly revealed in its wholeness and stops full length in one revolting piece. Just here in front. *No no! Go on! This is not the house!* And it never stopped arriving.

It was late in June of 1957. I was at home alone one evening when Ulla telephoned. Her voice was tight and flat. "Kay is dead. An hour ago. Come." I got there hurrying and breathless, then stumbled and nearly fell in shock. He was sitting in his chair, if it was Kay at all who sat there. He had just died, he had died within the hour. How could so much change overtake a man in so short a time? For a second he looked like one of the familiar figures in his books, but become ghastly. Next he seemed to be transparent and I was staring through his body and he was turning into crystals. It was not abomination that so quickly took over, but as the heart no longer beat and the blood no longer ran and neither could give him any stingy warmth, the snows and frost of dissolution began to consume him and the climate of absolute cold closed over him. In a southern latitude he was returning to his northern origins, his northern terminal, riding not with punctilio in a silver sleigh but seated heart-rending and sharp-nosed, quite upright in the same old padded chair.

I tried to speak to Ulla but she moved toward Kay and stood beside him. "Kay darling," she said in a wheedling way, "this is a brutal country. I want to keep you here with me with flowers all around in the house, and friends to come for that goodbye visit. A little while, a little while, Kay. But no. Brutal, savage, stupid. They'll be here at once to take you away. Is it all right with you, Kay?" She turned and listened and went to the door. "Already." She spoke helplessly and angrily. There was the sound of tires on the gravel drive. I went into the kitchen and found a few neighbors standing there, gazing sadly down at the floor. The Nielsens' Chinese physician came at that moment from the city and he joined us. We were all silent until the car drove away. "You will stay here with her tonight," the doctor said, speaking to no one in particular until his eyes met mine, "she is a danger to herself." We went back into the living room where Ulla stood, a figure of wax, or wood, or lead, not weeping, not losing her composure. "They took him away. What kind of savage law is that?" And she looked at each one of us in turn with contempt.

The doctor, about to leave for Los Angeles, administered a heavy dose of sedation. But she did not sleep. If I myself slept at all, I could not recall by morning. All night, until well after dawn, Ulla walked. She walked through a labyrinth of countless turnings, twistings, crossings, and at every crossing she looked for Kay, the living Kay, only to find him dead in his chair. She walked from room to room, endlessly, a long walk through the small house. Not once did I hear her cry out or even sob.

For several days he lay in an establishment in Pasadena surrounded by continually refreshened flowers while Ulla, still without tears, stood beside him and welcomed their friends as to a social function. His funeral took place at the large First Congregational Church in Los Angeles where his painting of the Twenty-third Psalm hung over the altar of the Wong Chapel. The shepherd, taking his enormous, long-legged stride up the cliff seemed to be climbing out of the funeral into the sky. Kay had belonged to the Danish Royal Guard. Ulla had not invited them, but members came to take part in the services. They marched down the aisle to carry their imposing flag and stand about their comrade. Ulla sat at the front of the chapel, in black, of course, and wearing a dingy black hat she had found in the closet. As though she had eyes in the back of her head she rose slowly at exactly the right moment as the big flag swung toward her, her round short figure bearing all the majesty and grief a woman can suffer at such a moment.

Kay was gone and no one doubted Ulla's desperation but she never made a mournful sound of any sort. If there existed then, or still, a shoulder she wept on, I do not know its name. A few kind but mistaken people tried to plan for her, assuming that she must in some way support herself.

She wanted no occupation at all for it would take her from home and where she could not see Kay's chair. The idea that she planned to make gestures of staying alive without Kay was an outrageous error on the part of friendly fools. Without any effort to be secret or withdrawn she simply continued to exist, but with no desire for it, and no intention to promote the belief that continuing to live was to be taken seriously. Once only she made a noticeable step toward social life. The Danish Ambassador was coming to Los Angeles and the Danish colony was to meet him at an important function in one of the large hotels. Ulla's pride forced her to attend. Kay's widow could not stay at home on such a night. She hunted up an antique evening dress and made it over until it had style. In her refurbished black lace, her strand of pearls and her good diamonds — never unwisely sacrificed in times of need — she was a lady, and the right occasion waited. But she was timid about going alone. "First my father took me. Then Kay took me. I have never gone anywhere alone." She faltered but she went, and the next day she reported the event with dramatic pleasure. "How did the great affair go?" I enquired. "The Ambassador," she answered, holding her head high, "saw me arrive, and he came the entire length of the huge ballroom to kiss my hand."

It occurred to me to take a poem to her that I thought would be right, and it was; Waley's translation of General Su Wu's farewell to his wife. Ulla went through the poem slowly. She saw the General off to cold frontiers and battle-grounds, and nodded sadly, and handed the book to me. "Please read the lovely last lines aloud." I read them — lines written twenty centuries ago:

> With all your might enjoy the spring flowers,
> But do not forget the time of our love and pride.
> Know that if I live I will come back again,
> And if I die, we will go on thinking of each other.

She was silent. "Poets know how to cope." "And some of them over-cope," I answered. "Not dear old Su Wu," she said positively and warmly. And we sat and passed the poem back and forth to each other and read it four times.

One day, going to see Ulla I was aware of her voice as I stepped onto the porch. Knocking and going into the house I saw that she was alone, and I knew that she had been talking to Kay and had been talking to him most of the time since he died. So she continued their existence together, and she could go on managing, as if for him, and asking his advice about what she must do, what and how and when. The way it always was. I saw nothing disturbing in this conference with the dead. She lived close to the edge, she had become an edge of living, a verge, a brink, ready to go over or beyond. To be on the verge as she was seemed a definable condition, even a kind of security.

Some sixty or seventy miles down the coast near the town of Laguna was a protected beach where Kay and Ulla had frequently gone to swim and picnic. On a warm day in late December Ulla took the poodle and went there. She told me about it afterward. She did not quite tell me all, but she did not have to tell me all. Commanding the dog to sit on the beach she went into the water. She waded out and out and began to swim. This was the way to get to Kay. This would end the foolishness of trying to accept too slowly the last of life in which there was no further reason for effort or existence. This was what they had planned. Or near enough.

Caught in the intensity and drag of the waves she began to give in to the mighty thrash and pull of water taking her farther and farther from land. She was an experienced swimmer, she knew the ocean was drawing her beyond return. Then she caught sight of the dog on the sand. He had stayed where she told him to stay, but he was frantic, rising and barking, sitting down and jumping up to yelp and implore. "I couldn't hear him bark," Ulla told me, "The waves had taken me so far. I could only see him, I could see how he was trying to make me hear, I could see how he was crazy with fear." She said nothing for a moment. "It was terrible, trying to come back. Once or twice I was certain I couldn't do it. I began to be very frightened. But the dog. The dog begging me to come back. At last I made it to the shore, and I crawled out. I lay there a long time, and he was crying all over me." "Ulla, oh, Ulla, Thank God you got back!" The ardor in my voice touched her. Besides, I was crying also, like the dog. Ulla put her arm around me as she said, "You really are a dear sweet idiot. Do you think I would go away and leave The Little Old Man there by the ocean all alone?" She smiled. She even tried to laugh. Ulla's true laugh was delectable and teasing, with a kind of chime in it. She was no good at an imitation. She was well aware that I knew just six months had passed since Kay's death.

And there was no further promise to keep her. She thought about it. About little else. She talked about it, to Kay, and to the dog. The dog listened fondly, and then he would go to sleep. At first he had missed Kay. Now he was used to being alone with Ulla, one world instead of two. She had an opportunity to discuss her problem with the Holy Spirit, for a religious neighbor tried to bring her the good news of God's continuing grace for the faithful. But she argued with him mercilessly and sent him on his way. She preferred her own profane beliefs, her own haunted skepticism. There were days when she was weak and ill. Had she not worn herself out with the harsh questions of her debate? She was positive that Kay could not cease to exist. But in what form did he continue? In every form his talent had taken, of course. But naturally. And in no other? In no way that could be met again, touched, embraced? Why did humanity believe with famish and hope in the going on of life after death? All the old passionate clichés came to reassure and nag her. For universal faith there must be a universal reason. The flowers we bring today are for loss and longing, but they stand for all those naive and useful gifts of food and comfort that furnished the graves of antiquity for the next life certain to be there. Not to mention the slaughtered slaves who went into the master's grave to serve him,

and the beautiful slain Scythian horses for him to ride and terrify new enemies. Why was she, the most loyal and clever of slaves, and as well-bred as a good horse, left behind? And she spoke in bitter praise of the Indian custom of suttee. And while she sat and stared at the empty chair the time was passing and no one, she would say, has ever come back to tell us a damn thing about what really happens. If it is as bad as life itself can be, well then . . . and she would lose her way. What stayed overwhelmingly in her mind was the memory of that terrifying ride the night they were followed along the steep cliff road with the black drop below into horror and extinction, there where the eternal waters of the ocean rose up with all their tides to take her, to take them both, the same waters she had barely escaped at the beach.

One day she requested, "Tell me again how the old poem ended." I hunted for it and found it in my head, "And if I die, we will go on thinking of each other." "That's a great deal," she said faintly, "soon it will be thirty-four years." I guessed what she meant. "Was it a beautiful wedding, Ulla?" "Quite possibly. And I was twenty-two." Then she added inconsequentially, "Let's give a party. Let's invite old Su Wu and his wife. But first I must make a will. Certain things to certain people." She forgot to make a will, she had no strength for it.

Soon after that I returned home after a few hours absence to learn that Erma had taken her by ambulance to a hospital in Los Angeles. Zoe called to tell me. "We were talking on the telephone. It became difficult. She could scarcely speak. I could hardly hear her. She was drifting. It's terrible, all this time she had failed to take the insulin. Nobody knew." And again, after an hour or two, "We don't know what can be done for her." And later, "Do you know? Just a year and a month since Kay died." "And three weeks," I added, "longer than she intended."

Early next morning I went to Ulla's house. Erma was feeding the poodle. I stood there. A small and pathetic place to hold so much that was uncommonly civilized and choice. Here had originated the three murals and the altar painting that would some day be possessively discovered by people of the west coast. Here the brilliant luxuries of "A Thousand and One Nights" had been lifted from the heavy wooden box, revealed, and then carefully returned and the lid shut down and the clasps secured, but not forever, I was confident. And what else? I saw Kay's easel and drawing board and on the board was lightly tacked a little wreath of boxwood from a bush in the garden. Without hesitation I took it. Certain things to certain people. A circle of brown stem with dry leaves still perfect, it was the natural form of elegy. I have kept it over the years. It has never lost its shape.

Hildegarde Flanner

(1) PROLOGUE

The Sultan of all India and China returns from
hunting early and discovers his wife with a black slave.
In a rage he has his wife, the slave and all his harem
executed. He then goes off to roam the world.

(2) Detail of the Sultan of all India and China hunting.

(3) PROLOGUE

On his travels the Sultan meets a beautiful girl who is
the captive of a Genie. The Genie keeps her locked
in a box, but around her neck is a little purse of rings
she has been given by other men despite the Genie's
precautions.

(4) Detail of the beautiful girl with her purse of rings.

(5) PROLOGUE

The Sultan returns to his kingdom completely
disillusioned. Having sworn never to trust another
woman, each night he takes a new bride and each
dawn he has her killed.
Scheherazade, the daughter of the Vizier, volunteers
to become the next bride. She has a plan to stop this
terrible destruction. At bedtime she starts to tell a tale
cleverly weaving the beginning of a second into the end
so that she must continue the next evening. In this
way she is reprieved for a thousand and one nights
and wins the Sultan's heart.

(6) Detail of Scheherazade telling her tale.

(7) THE TALE OF THE LITTLE HUNCHBACK

The Tailor, the Physician, the Steward and the
Merchant each think they are responsible for the
death of the little Hunchback, but each is saved from
hanging by the confession of the next. Just as the
Caliph is about to pass sentence the little Hunchback
sits up very much alive and says, 'I only had a fishbone
stuck in my throat!'.

(8) *Detail from* THE TALE OF THE LITTLE HUNCHBACK

(9) THE TAILOR'S TALE OF THE LAME YOUNG MAN AND
THE BARBER OF BAGHDAD FROM THE TALE OF THE
LITTLE HUNCHBACK

While taking a walk a young man sees a beautiful
young woman at a window watering some flowers and
he immediately falls in love with her.

(10) *Detail from* THE TAILOR'S TALE

(11) THE BARBER'S TALE OF HIS SECOND BROTHER FROM
THE TALE OF THE LITTLE HUNCHBACK

Ali Haddar is tricked by the Merchant's wife with
whom he is infatuated. She paints his face and
undresses him, then runs away. He chases after her only
to find himself naked in the marketplace. His right ear
is cut off for exposing himself in this way.

(12) *Detail from* THE BARBER'S TALE

(13) THE PHYSICIAN'S TALE OF A YOUNG MAN LOVED BY
TWO SISTERS FROM THE TALE OF THE LITTLE HUNCHBACK

While he sleeps with one sister the other slips into the
bedroom and kills her sister, hiding the wound with a
necklace of large pearls.

(14) *Detail from* THE PHYSICIAN'S TALE

(15) THE MERCHANT'S TALE OF THE YOUNG THIEF FROM
THE TALE OF THE LITTLE HUNCHBACK

A young man in love with a beautiful woman steals to
buy her luxuries, he is caught and his right hand is cut
off. To conceal this from her he must take the cup of
wine she offers with his left hand.

(16) *Detail from* THE MERCHANT'S TALE

(17) THE STEWARD'S TALE OF THE SULTAN'S WIFE'S
FAVORITE FROM THE TALE OF THE LITTLE HUNCHBACK

The Favorite falls in love with a young man and so
that she can smuggle him into the harem she hides him
in a box among some presents for the Sultan's wife.

(18) *Detail from* THE STEWARD'S TALE

(19) THE TALE OF KING YUNAN AND DUBAN THE DOCTOR
FROM THE TALE OF THE FISHERMAN AND THE GENIE

Duban cures the King of leprosy, but the ungrateful
King has him beheaded. Before he dies he tells the
King to place his head over a special book and he will
then be able to answer all the King's questions. This
the King does, but when he licks his fingers to turn the
pages, which have been poisoned, he dies.

(20) *Detail from* THE TALE OF KING YUNAN

(21) THE TALE OF KING SINDBAD AND THE FALCON FROM
THE TALE OF THE FISHERMAN AND THE GENIE

While out hunting the King being thirsty attempts to
drink from a stream running down a tree. Each time he
tries to drink his falcon knocks the cup from his hand.
After the third time the King cuts off the falcon's wing,
only then he discovers that the stream comes from the
mouth of a poisonous snake. The King carries the
falcon home where it dies in honour.

(22) *Detail from* THE TALE OF KING SINDBAD

(23) THE TALE OF THE ENCHANTED KING OF THE BLACK
ISLANDS FROM THE TALE OF THE FISHERMAN AND THE
GENIE

The young king loves his wife but she is a wicked
sorceress in love with a black slave. He discovers them
and wounds the slave. She turns the king into stone
from the waist down and beats him nightly to punish
him before going to visit her lover.

(24) *Detail from* THE TALE OF THE ENCHANTED KING

(25) THE TALE OF THE FIRST DERVISH FROM THE TALE
OF THE PORTER AND THE THREE GIRLS OF BAGHDAD

The Dervish's cousin is in love with his sister. They
have been forbidden to meet. He takes her to a
graveyard where he has built a vault where they can
be together. He asks his cousin to close the hidden
entrance after them.

(26) *Detail from* THE TALE OF THE FIRST DERVISH

(27) THE TALE OF THE FIRST DERVISH FROM THE TALE
OF THE PORTER AND THE THREE GIRLS OF BAGHDAD

The Dervish's cousin and his sister hidden in their
vault under the earth perish in the fire of the Almighty's
anger.

(28) *Detail from* THE TALE OF THE FIRST DERVISH

(29) THE TALE OF THE SECOND DERVISH FROM THE TALE
OF THE PORTER AND THE THREE GIRLS OF BAGHDAD

A Genie steals the daughter of the King of the Ebony
Isles on her wedding night.

(30) *Detail from* THE TALE OF THE SECOND DERVISH

(31) THE TALE OF THE THIRD DERVISH FROM THE TALE
OF THE PORTER AND THE THREE GIRLS OF BAGHDAD

This Dervish is told to sew himself into a sheepskin so
that the Roc will mistake him for a sheep and carry him
away. Then, when over a certain high rock to cut
himself out of the bag and frighten the Roc away.
And from there he will be able to see the castle
whither he is to go.

(32) *Detail from* THE TALE OF THE THIRD DERVISH

(33) THE TALE OF THE THIRD DERVISH FROM THE TALE
OF THE PORTER AND THE THREE GIRLS OF BAGHDAD

Arriving at the Castle he lives happily with the forty
young women he finds there, until one day when they
must leave him. They give him the keys, forbidding
him only one room. He eventually yields to temptation
and enters the room. He finds a magnificent black horse,
he mounts it and it carries him away from the castle
back to the brass tower from which he started.

(34) *Detail from* THE TALE OF THE THIRD DERVISH

(35) THE TALE OF THE FIRST GIRL FROM THE TALE
OF THE PORTER AND THE THREE GIRLS OF BAGHDAD

The girl is shipwrecked on an island where she enters a
castle to discover that the Queen and all her court
have been turned to stone for falling from the true
faith – except for one young man she finds reading the
Koran. They fall in love and sail away.

(36) *Detail from* THE TALE OF THE FIRST GIRL

(37) THE HISTORY OF NOUREDDIN ALI AND BEDREDDIN
HASSAN

Noureddin Ali and his older brother Shemseddin
Mohammed, both Viziers to the Sultan of Egypt sit
down one evening to plan their future. They agree to
marry two sisters from a good family and that their
wives shall conceive and bear children on the same day,
a son for one, a daughter for the other, but very soon
they argue over the size of the dowry and marriage
portion.

(38) *Detail from* THE HISTORY OF NOUREDDIN ALI AND
BEDREDDIN HASSAN

(39) THE HISTORY OF NOUREDDIN ALI AND BEDREDDIN
HASSAN

The Genie turns himself into a water buffalo to frighten
the hunchback bridegroom and keep him away from
the bridal chamber so that Bedreddin Hassan can
spend the night with his cousin, Shemreddin's daughter.

(40) *Detail from* THE HISTORY OF NOUREDDIN ALI AND
BEDREDDIN HASSAN

(41) THE HISTORY OF NOUREDDIN ALI AND BEDREDDIN
HASSAN

Bedreddin Hassan enters the bridal chamber of his
cousin, undresses and tells her that he is really her
bridegroom and the hunchback had been a joke played
by the Sultan on her father. Outside the Genie and the
Fairy listen and wait to steal him away and carry him
off to Damascus.

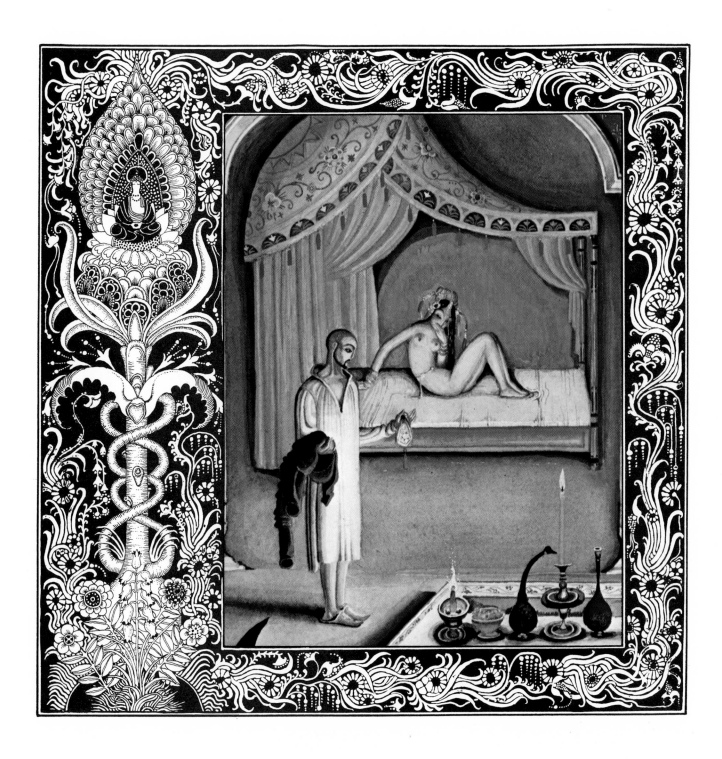

(42) *Detail from* THE HISTORY OF NOUREDDIN ALI AND
BEDREDDIN HASSAN

PEACOCK PRESS IS PROUD TO PRESENT THE FOLLOWING LIST:

HOWARD PYLE

ARTHUR RACKHAM

KAY NIELSEN (Book 1)

THE UNKNOWN PAINTINGS OF KAY NIELSEN (Book 2)

THE ENGLISH DREAMERS

EDMUND DULAC

THE FANTASTIC ART OF FRANK FRAZETTA (Book 1)

FRANK FRAZETTA: BOOK TWO

TEMPTATION

THE CHRISTMAS BOOK

THE FANTASTIC CREATURES OF EDWARD JULIUS DETMOLD

THE FANTASTIC WORLD OF GERVASIO GALLARDO

THE FANTASTIC ART OF CHARLES AND WILLIAM HEATH ROBINSON

ONCE UPON A TIME

Send for full catalogue
and price list from:
CASH SALES DEPT., BANTAM BOOKS
666 5th Avenue
New York, N.Y. 10019